ETERNALLY REFLECTING

Driving Your Memoir Forward
by Reflecting Back

The Workbook

by Amy Liz Harrison

alh

AMY LIZ HARRISON

A TEAM PRESS

About the Author

WELCOME

By Amy Liz Harrison

Amy Liz Harrison is a bestselling author, podcaster, and mother of eight who writes books for both kids and adults. Sober since 2011, Harrison's memoir series takes an honest look at her past drinking and road to recovery, her diagnosis with ADHD as an adult, and navigating life as an unapologetically awkward person.

Her decades of experience parenting through adversity inspired her to create a kid's book series about mental health. A former high school English teacher, she holds a Bachelor's in Communication from Azusa Pacific University and lives with her husband, who she married in 1998 after knowing him for five months, and their brood in Bellevue, Washington.

also by the Author

Harrison's first book, "**Eternally Expecting: A Mom of Eight Gets Sober and Gives Birth to a Whole New Life...Her Own**," details Harrison's journey from alcoholism to recovery, demanding she remain true to herself and her voice. However, she struggled to find talented individuals who supported her vision for the work. She ultimately produced a bestselling book and made many personal and professional connections along the way.

In the spirit of eternally evolving, Harrison immediately began work on her second book, "**Eternally Awkward: A Future Mom of Eight Reflects on Mysteries of Anxiety, ADHD and Coming of Age in the 80s.**" She gathered the most talented team members she met while creating her first book and discovered amazing new people with a variety of skills, and thus, the A-Team Press was born.

As a mother and a writer, Harrison felt inspired to create the "Kiss Your Brain" series of children's books in 2023. This series tackles the big mental health topics her family—and all families—face. With five stories written from a child's point of view, this series addresses substance abuse, eating disorders, and other mental health issues in a way that appeals to even the littlest readers.

This is to be used alongside Amy's Memoir Writing Workshop available on A-Team Press.com

A-Team Press is a publishing collective that supports independent authors founded by bestselling author Amy Liz Harrison in 2022. We offer opportunities to connect with other creators and talented small businesses to help with every phase of publishing your book. Learn more about Amy's Memoir Writing Course and our services

Did You Know?

This workbook was developed alongside bestselling author Amy Liz Harrison's 10-week Eternally Reflecting Memoir Class. Using her experience publishing two successful memoirs, Harrison created this workbook as resource to guide other writers through the process of sharing their stories with the world.

A message from the author:
"Memoir writing has been an amazing journey for me—I get to share my experience driving this road, while encouraging and connecting with others. I get to take the lessons I have learned from all the detours and wrong turns and leave my own guide book, forever emblazoned in my own words.
Join me in this adventure! Think of writing a memoir as a gift to yourself. When you realize the dark past is actually your greatest asset, you give yourself a priceless treasure: true emotional freedom."

Visit **A-teampress.com** to learn more about our writing coaching services.

Meet the CEO

Amy Liz Harrison

- Founder and CEO of A-Team Press
- Bestselling Memoir
- Number 3 in the works
- Hosts of the Eternally Amy Podcast
- Recovery Advocate

Meet The A-Team Press Team

Amy Liz Harrison
Author & CEO of A-Team Press

Carolyn Bunn
Business Management & Marketing

Becky Sasso
Book Editor

Angelica Watts
Administration & PR

Table of Contents

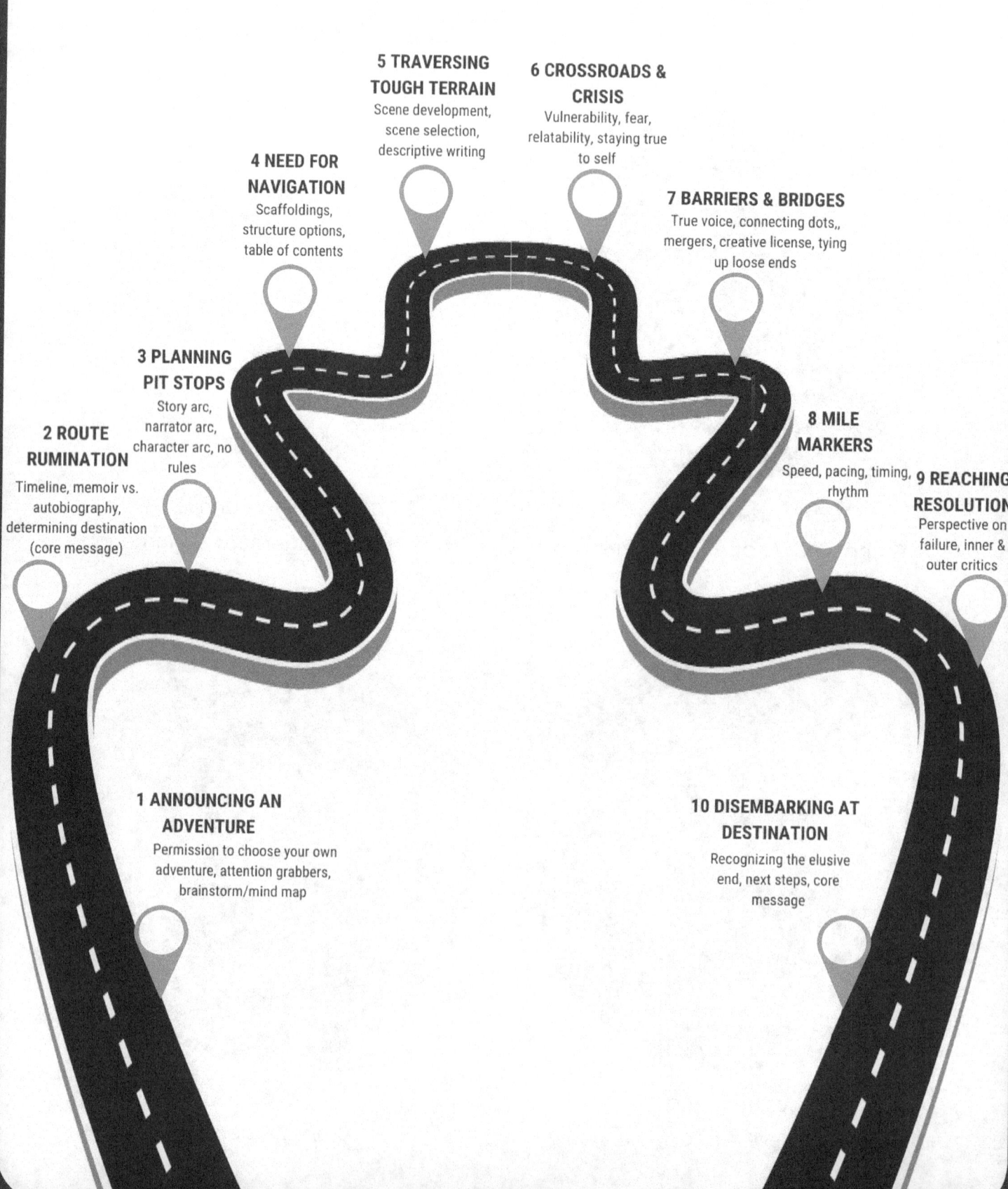

1: Announcing an Adventure

Letter from the Author

"Why didn't you just create a fictional character, whose personality is similar to yours, whose life is loosely based on your own journey, but no one has to know it's you? Why not do that and protect your dignity?"

Until a loud woman driving a mobility scooter asked me this exact question, protecting my personal anonymity never crossed my mind while writing my memoirs. Partially, it's because I'm proud of my journey and all I survived. But more than that—I want to leave the road map of my life behind in my own words. I don't want my adventures, crossroads, mile markers, and destinations left to the perceptions of others. I don't want my story interpreted, then passed along to my kids, and their kids, and the generation after that, like a tattered and coffee-stained Thomas Guide of my life.

"There's only one driver behind the wheel of my story—that's me. And now that I've come over rocky terrain out the other side of the tragedies and agonies of defeat, to a beautiful destination, I know one clear purpose in my life. I am meant to share my badass story so others can recognize that they, too, have a journey of unique and inspiring badassery.

Memoir writing has been an amazing journey for me—I get to share my experience driving this road, while encouraging and connecting with others. I get to take the lessons I have learned from all the detours and wrong turns and leave my own guide book, forever emblazoned in my own words.

Join me in this adventure! Think of writing a memoir as a gift to yourself. When you realize the dark past is actually your greatest asset, you give yourself a priceless treasure: true emotional freedom.

—Gratefully, ALH

2: Route Rumination

"Authors do not choose a story to write, the story chooses us."

—Richard P. Denney

Overview

Welcome to the beginning of your memoir writing adventure!

In this chapter, we will dive into the art of capturing your readers' attention right from the very first chapter and identifying your core message. Think of it as laying out the road map for the trip you're about to take them on.

Understanding the distinction between a memoir and an autobiography is essential. While an autobiography provides a comprehensive overview of a person's life, a memoir is a focused slice, a specific chapter.

Writing a memoir means your experiences are generally focused around a specific portion of your life (e.g., a high school experience; a 10-year marriage, etc.).

Writing an autobiography means your story includes the nuts and bolts of your life – cradle to the grave. Autobiographies are usually unemotional in nature due to it being such a broad overview.

Imagine your core message as your destination and the narrative style you choose as the vehicle to reach it. Consider which approach aligns better with your story. There are no rigid rules, just your choice. You're in control here.

A memoir is more than just a recounting of events; it's a powerful way to communicate emotions, lessons, thoughts, and experiences. The adventure of writing a memoir will last through the entire journey from start to finish.

Some parts aren't fun to write and recounting past experiences may be difficult, but they are needed to tell our stories.

Writing Prompt

What do you want your readers, your passengers, to experience as they join you on this literary journey?

_____

_____

_____

_____

_____

_____

_____

_____

_____

_____

_____

_____

_____

_____

_____

_____

_____

_____

Creating Your Story's Hook

Crafting an attention-grabbing first chapter is like captivating your reader at the starting line of a thrilling race.

You're the expert in your story. You know what you've experienced, even though some of your readers may not. Use your personal experiences as an authority voice to connect with them on a profound level.

Use sensory details, foreshadowing, and vivid descriptions to draw readers into your world. Show, don't tell them what's happening. Paint a picture of your emotions, thoughts, and experiences. Remember, your readers are here to experience your journey through your eyes.

Descriptive wording, foreshadowing, and flashbacks help to create a compelling first chapter. Flashbacks are especially powerful tools for connecting your readers to your past experiences. With these, you can weave past and present events to create a multi-dimensional narrative for readers.

Example of how powerful descriptive wording can be in *Song of the Plains: A Memoir of Family, Secrets, and Silence* by Linda Joy Myers:

"It's more than eyes and hair. The curve of a cheek. The shape of a lip. A smile. A happy temperament. We inherit many things in our genes. But here's a question: how much is nature vs nurture?"

Myers shares her generational experiences and ties them together in the beginning of the memoir to begin her story. She was raised by another family member instead of her own mother, and her mother also experienced the same exact thing.

Example of captivating attention grabbers using authority of voice in *Drinking: A Love Story* by Carolyn Knapp:

"The comfort was enormous. It was an easier, stronger version of myself. As though I've been coated by the inside out with warm armor, it's true. It's a statement of fact. Alcohol was the key to that feeling."

Knapp paints a picture for us about her experience with alcoholism. She made matter-of-fact statements and asserted her authority and knowing in this space.

Trip Planner Worksheet: Mapping Your Memoir Journey

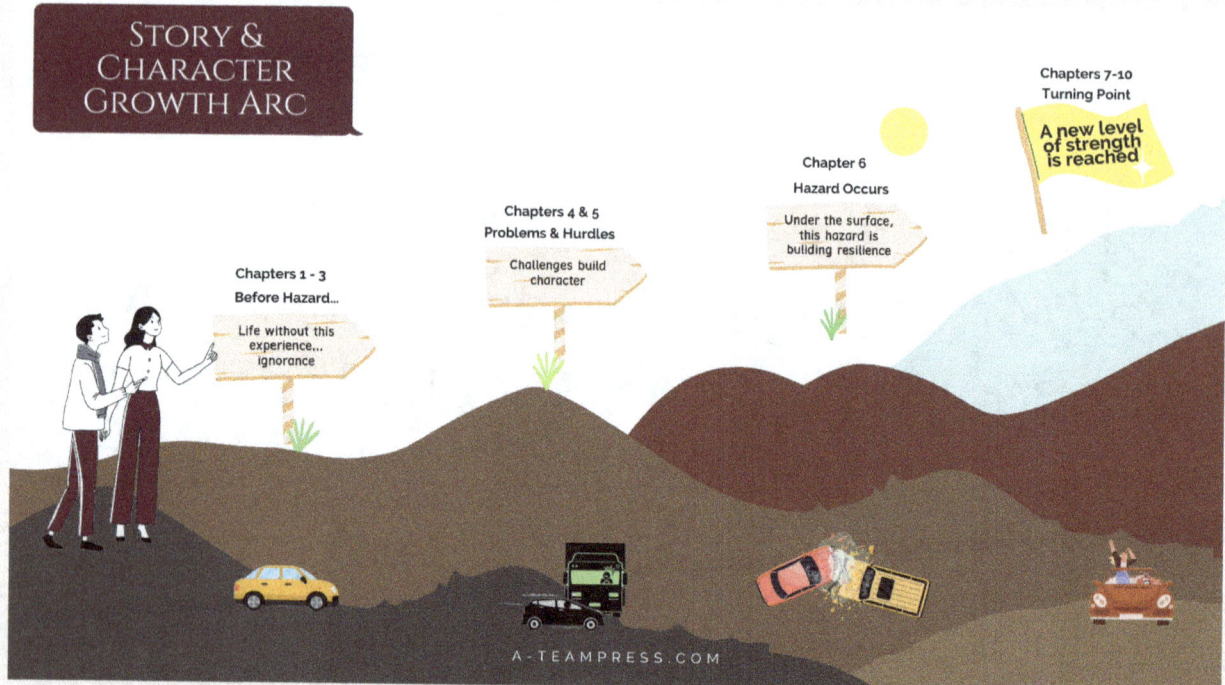

Our Trip Planner worksheet will be your guide as you map out the significant points in your life. These anchor points will create a structured path for your memoir, helping you stay focused and on track as you navigate the twists and turns of your memories.

Writing Prompt

Reflect on your core message and jot down initial thoughts on how you'll craft your first chapter to create a powerful and intriguing start.

_____

_____

_____

_____

_____

_____

_____

_____

_____

_____

_____

_____

_____

_____

_____

_____

3: Planning Pit Stops

"Start writing, no matter what.
The water does not flow until the
faucet is turned on."

—Louis L'Amour

Narrator Arcs vs Character Arcs

While both narrator arcs and character arcs are essential components of storytelling, they serve distinct purposes within your memoir.

A narrator arc encapsulates the entire progression of your story, from the inception to the resolution, providing a comprehensive journey for your readers. On the other hand, a character arc is a recurring theme that hones in on a specific experience, often grounded in relatable human emotions.

A character arc is your opportunity to highlight the key experiences that define your memoir's core message. Work backward from your destination, reflecting on the life experiences that led you to where you are now. From there, identify the conflict within these experiences, as they will form the foundation of your mini-arcs, which adds depth and resonance to your story.

As you craft your character arc, consider the elements that will build the rising action of your story. This climactic moment should be connected to the themes you introduced in Chapter 1. It's where your journey reaches its peak and your growth shines through to readers.

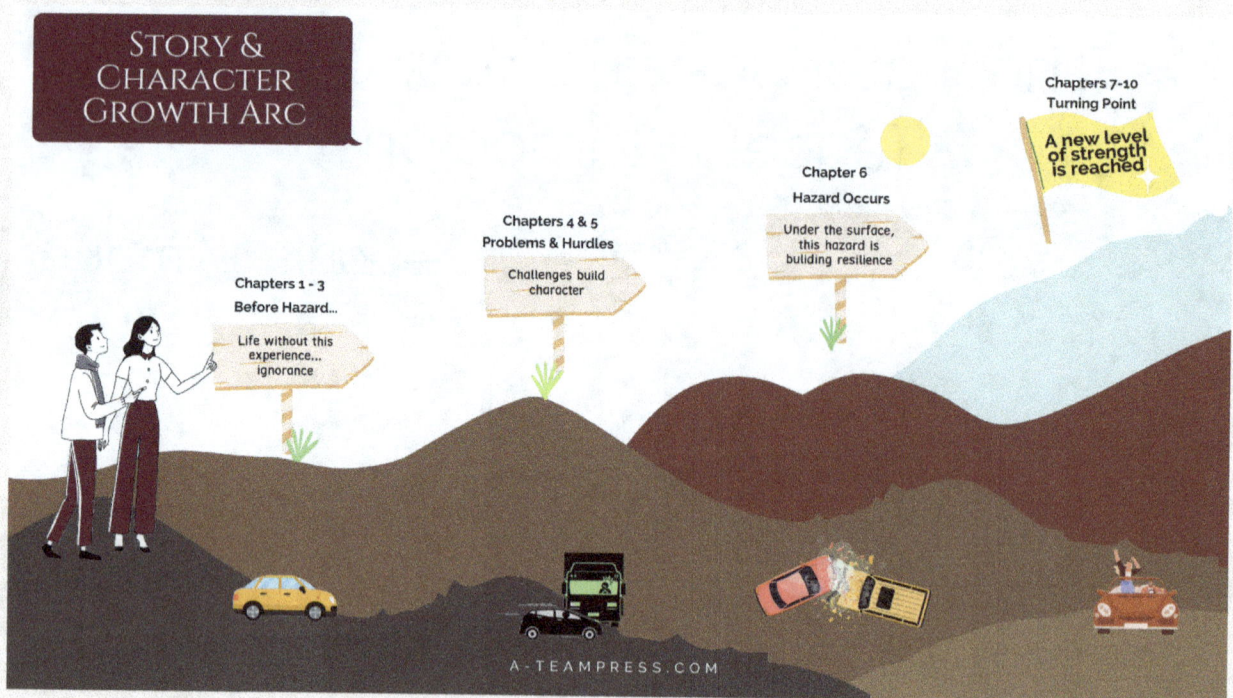

STORY & CHARACTER GROWTH ARC

Chapters 1 - 3
Before Hazard...
Life without this experience... ignorance

Chapters 4 & 5
Problems & Hurdles
Challenges build character

Chapter 6
Hazard Occurs
Under the surface, this hazard is building resilience

Chapters 7-10
Turning Point
A new level of strength is reached

A-TEAMPRESS.COM

The Seven Basic Story Plots

_____

_____

_____

_____

_____

_____

_____

_____

_____

Feel free to explore using elements from the 7 different basic story plot structures. From the heroic journey of overcoming "monsters" to the tale of rebirth and transformation like in *Beauty and the Beast*, these add structure to your story and help readers relate.

The hero's journey is a timeless story plot you can include in your memoir that mirrors a familiar human experience. It takes readers through a departure, an adventure into the unknown, a problem or monster to overcome, and eventual triumph and self-discovery.

Writing prompt

Fill in the Story & Character Growth Worksheet below to map out Chapters 1 - 10 of your memoir. Be sure to include events and experiences that are connected and part of both your story and character arcs.

STORY &
CHARACTER
GROWTH ARC

Chapters 1 - 3
Before Hazard...

Life without this
experience...
ignorance

Chapters 4 & 5
Problems & Hurdles

Challenges build
character

Chapter 6
Hazard Occurs

Under the surface,
this hazard is
buliding resilience

Chapters 7-10
Turning Point

A new level
of strength
is reached

A-TEAMPRESS.COM

_____

_____

_____

_____

_____

_____

_____

_____

4: Need for Navigation

"And by the way, everything in life is writable if you have the outgoing guts to do it, and the imagination to improvise. The worst enemy to creativity is the self-doubt."

—Sylvia Plath

Overview

We talked about determining your destination (core message). Now let's look at the different vehicles you can use to reach it. Just as a traveler chooses a vehicle to navigate different terrains, you have an array of vehicles at your disposal that serve as the structure of your memoir's narrative. Each vehicle offers a unique way to transport your readers, shaping their experience and guiding them through your story. There are many vehicles you can choose from: Sedan, Hybrid, Electric Vehicle, Branded Company Truck, Convertible, and Conversion Van. Let's dive into each plot structure and how they're commonly used:

The Sedan Structure

The Sedan is the common plot structure for writing. It's a chronological story, usually taking passengers straight from Point A to Point B. It is not limited to a certain time period and is usually within a "now" trajectory.

The Convertible Structure

This structure is different from a Sedan in that it almost always covers a short period of time. It's done in chronological order with more than enough backstory and context woven in for the passengers.

The Hybrid Car Structure

The Hybrid Car plot weaves together two, sometimes three parallel timelines. An example of a Hybrid plot would be

The Electric Vehicle Structure

With an Electric Vehicle structure, there is a central episode at the heart of your memoir. Throughout your memoir, you'll make departures to explore the terrain of the story, but for the point of informing your passengers of the central episode at the heart of the memoir.

The Branded Company Truck Structure

When using the Branded Company Truck structure, you're using associations to move the reader through your book. Associations can be . Writers rely on turning points and big, thematic events to propel them forward. Examples of using the Branded Company Truck structure is.

The Conversion Van Structure

The Conversion Van structure is the most unconventional of the plot structures. This can be a combination of any of the other plot structures and for anything that falls outside of that.

Writing prompt

Reflect on which structure resonates most with your story and core message. Consider how each structure shapes the reader's experience and enhances your storytelling.

_____

_____

_____

_____

_____

_____

_____

_____

_____

_____

_____

_____

_____

_____

5: Traversing Tough Terrain

"Lock up your libraries if you like;
but there is no gate, no lock, no bolt
that you can set upon the freedom
of my mind."

—Virginia Woolf

Descriptive Writing and Scene Development

We're now in the nitty gritty of your writing where the scenes are greatly detailed using dialogue, descriptive writing, and transitions between scenes. Description is the heartbeat of your memoir, breathing life into otherwise mundane moments. The most boring memoirs in the world include scenes that lack description and fall flat with readers.

Scenes are the building blocks of your memoir, often comprising 3-6 per chapter. While there are no rules, scene development calls for a balance of knowing what to include and what to leave out. Be prepared to face challenges where scenes you've developed may not fit or are unnecessary. Discussing these with an editor can help you refine your narrative.

As you navigate developing your scenes, remember that seeking an outside perspective can be invaluable. Discussing your scenes with an editor, a writing friend, or a fellow writer allows fresh insights to shine light on areas where you may be too close to the story to see clearly.

Key Elements to Make Scenes Come Alive

Your memoir's scenes should be more than just words; they should be an experience.

As you paint your scenes, consider the passage of time and the significance of age. While context is essential for your readers, not every scene requires context especially if you're working on a chronological timeline.

Think about ways to describe what's happening for your reader using sensory details, thoughts, and emotions. The goal is to have them feel like they are in the scene with you, as if they are immersed in a VR-like experience.

Even the smallest details create feelings of connection and relatability. Sometimes we forget these little details because we know what we experienced, so we need to tell and show our passengers.

With traumatic experiences, we have to put ourselves back in this time and it can trigger negative emotions and feelings. In order to convey the depth of these feelings, you have to be able to build a bridge for empathy and connection to happen with your readers.

Examples of Dialogue and Narration

Narration example 1:

"We went to the store to get the wedding dress and then out for coffee afterwards. It was a nice afternoon."

This narration is more autobiographical and doesn't use much sensory detail. Therefore, it doesn't evoke true emotion with readers.

Narration example 2:

"After we made our selection, our hearts warm and our smiles wide, we decided to go celebrate the commencement of this new journey – Laura marrying the man of her dreams, the one she met for that brief moment in time at that crosswalk so many years ago. Quite serendipitously, we exited the store with boxes under our arms, only to gaze up and see the sign on the next storefront: in old English writing, with peeling daffodil colored paint were the words '*Crosswalk Coffee*.'"

You want the passenger to be woven into the moment you're sharing where they're feeling the tone and emotion you're trying to evoke. When creating dialogue and narration, your goal is to create a feeling and emotion that displays the nature of your scene.

Transitions

Transitions are like the sturdy bridges that you cross to connect scenes together. They also guide your readers through your story in a clear and cohesive way

As an author, you hold the compass that directs your readers' journey. After all, you're taking them on this literary road trip! You move your readers to a new place or experience, either physically or emotionally. This makes sure your readers are never lost and always knowing exactly where they are in your story.

You can use a paragraph break, page breaks, or new chapters to help transition between scenes, depending on where you are in your memoir writing.

For example, there's best-selling author Elizabeth Gilbert's, "Eat, Pray, Love" where Elizabeth seamlessly transitions from Italy to India to Indonesia using chapter breaks, making it clear and obvious exactly where the reader is in her story.

The ability to connect scenes is necessary for telling your story in a cohesive way that keeps the passenger with you and doesn't abandon them on the side of the road at the last stop.

The Rearview Mirror

Imagine the rearview mirror in your car – it reveals what's behind you, unseen by your passengers. Similarly, your memoir holds treasures of insight that only you possess. This is the most powerful gift you can give yourself and your readers – the rearview mirror.

Your rearview mirror in memoir writing is information that you are privy to and need to communicate with your passenger. You want to offer two perspectives to keep you on track of 1) who you WERE vs who you ARE and 2) the road to get there.

This can be both fun AND agonizing at times. It's completely normal to have feelings come up in this part of your story. As you traverse this tough terrain, know that you are on track. This is exactly where the rubber meets the road.

If your memory is a bit foggy, or you can't remember every little detail - feel free to take creative license. This doesn't change your core message and that's all that matters.

Example of transition and transformation from my book, Eternally Expecting:

"Fred finally asked, "Aim-ee, what eez problem. Why you no stay so-bear?"
I shrugged and said I didn't think I was an alcoholic before all this mess. I looked off out the window at a large, middle aged woman walking a massive gang of yipping chihuahuas. I cannot feeks for you. You must feeks for yourself," Fred announced. Well, shit. I was afraid of that. My drinking had made a minefield of my life and here I was twiddling my thumbs expecting some poor soul to clean it all up – namely my parents, or my husband, or this guy. I really wasn't up for fixing my own issues."

This scene happens simultaneously as I narrate what's happened and what I learned from it that leads to a major transition. This is the moment I share my rearview mirror with my passenger

Writing Prompt

Using what you learned in this lesson, develop and bring a scene from your memoir to life using descriptive language, dialogue and transitions. Remember your rearview mirror!

_____

_____

_____

_____

_____

_____

_____

_____

_____

_____

_____

_____

_____

_____

_____

6: Crossroads and Crisis

"You don't write because you want to say something, you write because you have something to say."

—F. Scott Fitzgerald

Overview

We've now reached the crossroads of your memoir writing journey where moments of crisis and the voices of critics emerge. These critics take form as inner and outer critics, each influencing your narrative in different ways.

Your inner critics are the negative and self-limiting thoughts that you have about yourself. Oftentimes, these thoughts and beliefs may not even be your own. Outer critics are the projections and assumptions that challenge your objectivity. This is the worriedness you feel about how your classmates will perceive you, what faceless strangers will say online, and if your loved ones will judge you.

It's here where you must face those inner and outer critics and learn to discern constructive introspection from harmful self-sabotage. Ask if there may be any truth to what these critics are saying. This is not always the case and these may very well be projections with no substantial truth to it.

Writing Prompt

Allow your inner critic to voice its doubts, fears, and judgments about your writing. Share what negative thoughts or self-criticisms arise.

_____

_____

_____

_____

_____

_____

_____

_____

_____

_____

_____

_____

_____

_____

_____

_____

_____

Seeking Input vs Permission

Writing a memoir involves not only your memories but also the lives and experiences of others. Give high consideration to who you are including in your book. When considering whether to mention someone in your memoir, ask yourself: "*Would I be comfortable if someone wrote about me in this context?*" If the answer is no, you should seek permission.

Seeking permission involves getting consent from those you intend to mention. On the other hand, seeking input implies informing those involved without necessarily seeking their formal approval.

Memoirs often tread close to legal boundaries, especially when discussing crimes, personal issues, or sensitive matters. If you have any questions about including certain experiences involving other people, do your own research and consult a lawyer specializing in intellectual property and defamation.

Writing About Challenging Relationships

For those of us navigating actively healed or healing relationships, the process of writing a memoir centered around challenging relationships can be both challenging and transformative.

In Jeanette McCurty's memoir, "I'm Glad My Mom Died," she shares information about the traumatic childhood events and experiences she had with her mother. When her mom passes, she doesn't know who she is and she goes to therapy where she describes and then defends her mother's abuses to her therapist. She then realizes how freeing it felt to write and share her experiences without having to worry about her mother's reactions or responses.

At this stage in our writing, the inner critic—fueled by guilt and shame—becomes a constant companion and attempts to discourage us from exploring painful memories. It's important to remember that guilt is convicting, but shame is a limiting belief that keeps you stuck. The more you honor and give yourself permission to tell your story with truth and integrity, the more empowered you are.

Writing About Family and Close Relationships.

Frame experiences and events from your perspective so the passenger knows it's yours alone. Approach your family and close relationships, past or present, with empathy and understanding while also acknowledging that other perspectives exist.

This is where disclaimers may come in useful. Disclaimers give yourself the freedom to tell your story with authenticity using anonymous descriptions and pseudonyms. Understand that your experiences, even if they closely resemble others, are uniquely yours. If you lived through it, you have license to tell your story on your own terms.

Writing Prompt

Think about a significant relationship from your past that has left a lasting impact on your life. This could be a family member, a friend, a romantic partner, or anyone who has played a pivotal role in shaping your experiences.

Now, create a scene that involves this relationship and write about the interaction, event, or moment while employing the techniques we've covered.

_____

_____

_____

_____

_____

_____

_____

_____

_____

_____

_____

_____

_____

_____

7: Barriers and Bridges

The process of writing a memoir is about stepping into the light, confronting your past, and finding healing through the power of your own words."

—Maya Angelou

The Turning Point

Welcome to the climax of your memoir! At this point, you've presented your turning point and your true essence has been revealed. This is where your voice becomes more distinct and impactful. Your voice is the connection that lets your passengers understand what you've experienced and how they relate to it in their own way. Much like a "before and after" image, it evolves and matures throughout your memoir, shaping the evolution of your journey.

Voice as a Barrier

Your voice functions as both a bridge, connecting your story to your readers, and a potential barrier that adds depth and complexity. Some people don't know their own voice or are unfamiliar with it. Many people don't even like their own voice recordings, but eventually they get used to it. You can either choose to let this hold you back as a barrier, or you can use your voice as the bridge to create context and help get your reader on their way to the next intended destination.

The Impact of Voice in Memoirs

Voice should add style, energy, and a distinctive flair to your writing. It should be interesting enough to keep the reader engaged and enhance the story being told, and the overall tone. At this point, you should be able to look at different points in your story and determine what your tone will be for each scene. Keep in mind that while there are no set rules when writing your story, you should make your tone appropriate for what's happening while developing your scenes.

Voice Includes Choice

When writing a memoir, you have the power of choice. Your voice is not a fixed entity; it's dynamic and complex just like life's seasons. Wayne Dyer reminds us that "What worked then, doesn't work now." Embrace this mantra as you work through your memoir. Understand that you can change your voice (mind) throughout your memoir alongside your personal growth.

It's important to acknowledge that while you can wield choice with your voice, you may also inadvertently offend. You cannot control others' reactions to your words. Words that once resonated might become sensitive or inappropriate in the future. Yet, you possess the agency to choose your words and stay true to your experiences. Don't be swayed by the Grammar Police or the critique of others—your voice is yours, and you have the creative license to wield it as you see fit.

Within the spectrum of choice also lies the ability to be wrong, speculate, and even vacillate. Give yourself the gift of grace in these moments. Your memoir is a representation of your journey, complete with twists, turns, and uncertainties. The fluidity of your voice mirrors the ebbs and flows of life; allow yourself to explore and experiment and show this in your writing.

Example of using voice to convey emotion in "Know My Name" by Chanel Miller:

"Later, I was at my desk, sipping a mug of coffee, scrolling through a sandwich menu for lunch. I clicked back to the news on my homepage and saw, Stanford Athlete. Saw. raping. Saw. unconscious woman. I licked again. My screen filled with two blue eyes and a neat row of teeth. Freckles. Red tie. Black suit. I have never seen this man before. Brock Turner. I read he had been charged with 5 felony counts. I do not list them all here.

But the one includes "sexual assault with a foreign object" sticks out. Too many words jumbled together. Read it again slower. I typed into Google: What is a foreign object? The panic was quiet and slow. It was defined as an object that intrudes where it should not be intruding, as into a living body or machinery. Examples include: a speck of dust in the eye, a splinter, a woodchip, fish hook glass, and what intruded into me."

As readers, Miller's use of voice envelopes you into the scene. She uses incomplete sentences, interjections, statements, and slowed staccato pacing for observation and to jar the senses.

Example of using voice to speculate in "Untamed" by Glennon Doyle:

"10 years later, my fraternity boy will marry a woman I adore. He'll say that it took some time to get over our relationship. He'll say that, one night they were in an argument and they became distant. She'll say, what are you thinking about? He said, "Glennon. She just didn't give a fuck." Any woman who doesn't give a fuck is simply abandoning her soul to adhere the rules. No woman on Earth doesnt give a fuck. No woman is that cool. She's just hidden her fire. Likely, it's burning her up."

Doyle speculates all throughout her writing. She's imagining and speculating that this is how the scenario would unfold in the future. It is not necessarily what actually happens, but what she imagines in her head may happen.

Example of tone changing with age in "Heavy" by Kiese Laymon

"My body knew things my mouth and my mind couldn't or maybe wouldn't express. I knew that all over my neighborhood boys were trained to harm girls in ways girls could never harm boys. Straight kids were trained to harm queer kids in ways queer kids could never harm queer kids. Men were trained to harm women in ways women could never harm men. Parents were trained to harm children in ways children would never harm parents. Babysitters were trained to harm kids in ways that kids could never harm babysitters. My body knew white folks were trained to harm us in ways we could never harm them. I didn't know how to tell you or anyone else. The story is, my body told me. But like you, I knew how to run, deflect, and duck."

Laymon writes about his experiences as a 13 year old and what he knew then versus what he knows now.

Writing Prompt

Think about one moment in your memoir that holds significant personal meaning. Reflect on how you might have described this moment in your voice at that time—assertive, cautious, poetic, or perhaps even uncertain.

How would your voice evolve to convey the same experience today? Write a passage that captures both versions of your voice—past and present.

_____

_____

_____

_____

_____

_____

_____

_____

_____

_____

_____

_____

_____

_____

8: Mile Markers

"Writing a memoir is not about what happened to you; it's about your take on what happened to you."

—Roxane Gay

Overview

Many times during our memoir writing, our stories have their own unique cadence—alternating between slow, contemplative moments and brisk, exhilarating scenes. You may also have different tones, timeframes, and characters that are introduced throughout your memoir.

Keeping track of characters and storylines

The task of keeping track of multiple storylines, characters, and details can become overwhelming as you progress through your story. Consider using tools such as Scrivener or starting a spreadsheet to keep track of characters and details. Visual boards can also serve as a storyboard for your reference.

It's important to do this in order to show your passenger exactly where you are and to keep up a good pace throughout your memoir. They'll get to see all of the loose ends from your story tied up and will be able to keep up with how each detail and storyline is connected.

Transitioning your timing

Skipping time periods is a common struggle for writers. You can use chapter breaks to transport your passengers to the next chapter of your journey in a natural way, while still capturing the essence of your experiences. Events paragraphs are another useful way to transition your timing through your writing. This is a series of sentences that connect two separate events. As long as they relate, it's easy to slip this into your writing when you need to jump to another scene. You may also find that creating a premise with an obvious connector to transition your timing makes for a smooth transition between scenes.

You can use as many details that are connected as possible. From there, you may use creative license to create a flow with the pacing throughout your memoir. Go back through these details with an editor to make sure all connections make sense and are necessary to include for your core message.

Example of using page breaks in "Kitchen Confidential" by Anthony Bourdain

"I'd sit in the garden among the tomatoes and lizards and eat my oysters and drink coronaburgs. France was wonderful for underage drinkers. I still associate the taste of oysters with those heady wonderful days of illicit late afternoon buzzes, smell of french cigarettes, the taste of beer. That unforgettable feeling of doing something I shouldn't be doing..."

"It's 1973. I'm happily in love. I graduated high school a year early so I could chase the object of my desire to Vasser college. The less said about that part of my life, the better. Believe me. But suffice it to say that by age 18, I was a thoroughly undisciplined young man."

Example of using events paragraphs in "Educated" by Tara Westover:

"Months passed in this way. Mother leaving the house at all hours and coming home, trembling. Relieved that it was all over... By the time the leaves started to fall, she'd helped with a dozen births by the end of winter. Several deaths. In the Spring, she told my father she'd had enough."

Example of using events paragraphs in "Educated" by Tara Westover:

"Months passed in this way. Mother leaving the house at all hours and coming home, trembling. Relieved that it was all over... By the time the leaves started to fall, she'd helped with a dozen births by the end of winter. Several deaths. In the Spring, she told my father she'd had enough."

Example of creating a premise with an obvious connector to skip time in "Cup of Water Under My Bed" by Daisy Hernández:

"In high school, I tape a picture of an electric typewriter to the refrigerator and he buys it for me. The exact model and IBM written on it. He grins, watching me type my paper on Oscar Wilde on the playwright's time in prison for being gay. And this line from a poem hits, which I don't understand, but somehow makes sense to me: Each man kills the thing he loves. My father observes me for a few seconds spinning over the electronic typewriter then retreats to the kitchen for a can of Budweiser.

I enter the book publishing industry after college in the late 90s. I open mail for book editors, I write rejection letters and proofread flat copy. I spend day after day immersed in manuscripts and at the end of every two weeks, I'm paid on time."

Writing Prompt

Recall a pair of moments separated by time, yet linked by a common theme or emotion. Craft a premise with an obvious connector that bridges these moments.

_____

_____

_____

_____

_____

_____

_____

_____

_____

_____

_____

_____

_____

_____

_____

9: Reaching Resolution

"Write what should not be forgotten."

—Elizabeth Gilbert

Overview

As we near the end of our writing, a peculiar guest often sneaks in uninvited—the notorious Imposter Syndrome. It's that nagging doubt that questions your authenticity, your right to tell your story, and your place in the writing world. This is the moment where you must quit being at war and surrender to your writing. Stop telling yourself that you don't have an original story worth telling because it is far from the truth. Your perspective, your voice, and your experiences are valid and deserving of expression.

Copying and Remixes

Intellectual property is a complicated concept. Don't fear that you are copying because your story may contain elements of other people's stories. All of our experiences will have certain commonalities, like shared common feelings, thoughts, and memorable events. You'll commonly hear remixes, essentially copying, in new music where they sample older songs. They're typically created into a new song–sometimes entirely. That goes to say even if everything is remixed, it's never been said in YOUR voice and telling YOUR unique story.

Take Disney for example. Disney took stories like Pinocchio, Snow White and the Seven Dwarves, Sleeping Beauty, and Alice in Wonderland taken from public domain and recreated their own stories using animations. They went on to lobby for copyright terms afterwards.

Cultural Influences and Fair Use

Cultural norms are learned and passed down by watching and copying someone else. Almost everyone at some point was taught how to tie their shoes by watching someone else and copying them. Of course, we all have different variations of how we tie them, but we all learned the basic concepts and idea of how it's done. For my new book, *Moonwalkers*, I used Canva Pro and AI to create images which I altered to create my own illustrations, using a disclaimer that mentions images and elements have been altered.

We're all influenced by pop culture in some way and fair use is acceptable. In the back of my book, *Eternally Awkward*, there is a workbook with games and coloring pages that look like Highlights Magazine from the 80s. I didn't call it "Highlights Magazine," but I took the same concepts and it's inferred that I was influenced by the famous magazine. Of course, when it comes to intellectual property, please consult with a lawyer especially if you plan to use any references or have questions or concerns.

Adaptations and Rebrands

Memes are an example of copying: they're turned into adaptations of the original version of an image. This makes it into something entirely new in many cases. Sequels exist because we want a new, rebranded version of the old. It's part of the reason why we have so many Fast and Furious, Batman, and Godzilla movies. They all share the same concept, but each adaptation has a different storyline.

Predictable Arcs and Storylines

Superheroes typically have special abilities and overcome great life challenges and obstacles. We expect this with each different story. It's the most modern version of the hero's journey, but still the same concept is applied. You can see these similar arcs in books and movies like The Hunger Games, Avatar, The Shawshank Redemption, The Lion King, Harry Potter, and Lord of the Rings. Predictable arcs can be seen everywhere with the same concept. Similar plots and storylines are expected, but there are new characters with your story - YOU! This time, you are the superhero in your own story.

Writing Prompt

Write a scene using a predictable arc, the hero's journey, or adaptation of your favorite movie. This should be related to your memoir and may include other characters, pop culture influences, or familiar cultural norms.

_____

_____

_____

_____

_____

_____

_____

_____

_____

_____

_____

_____

_____

_____

_____

_____

10: Disembarking at Destination

"Writing a memoir is a profound journey of self-discovery. Embrace the vulnerability and let your truth shine."

—Elizabeth Gilbert

Overview

By now, you should know that you connected with your audience, showed your strengths and weaknesses, and delivered your core message that you wanted them to know by the end of your memoir. Ask yourself, "Did I take the passenger where I intended to go?" You want this to be the equivalent of parking your car at the giant 'Welcome' sign that is your core message.

Recognizing the End

You don't have to come up with a Quentin Tarantino-style ending. Your story has enough power on its own. End where it feels organic, naturally unforced, and complete. Consider whether you've come full circle with any details or moments you mentioned throughout your story. You may find extra assistance in doing this by getting outside help from a friend or editor if you have trouble tying up any loose ends at this point.

Writing for Yourself and Writing to Market

If we don't write for ourselves when writing a memoir, we're missing out on an authentic experience. Don't sell yourself short by focusing on sales and selling. Writing for yourself is generally therapeutic and the benefits are more than just profits. Writing to market or sell is a different thing. These types of memoirs are often false or fabricated using specific keywords with the intention to make it to a bestselling list. In the end, you'll make the best decision for yourself with whatever you choose to do.

There will be people who won't appreciate or identify with what you wrote. There may even be people who are upset by what you wrote. But for those who do appreciate, understand, and identify–it is WORTH IT.

Excerpt from "On Writing and Failure" by Stephen Marche

"In the best work, the intentions of the author fall away – leaving an open field for readers to play in. And they create meanings that may have nothing to do with the author's. Jonathan Swift famously intended Gulliver's travels as an indictment of all humanity, but ended up leaving a story for children… "Nobody knows what they're writing. Intention never aligns with result. You never know how readers will react. You never see how readers will react."

Embracing challenges and controlling only what you can control – like Prince!

Your readers will take what they will away from your memoir. Even if someone doesn't get it, you still want to make sure your core message is as clear as possible. Beyond that, you're not responsible for their interpretation. It may not be widely-accepted, but if you've done your best to stay true to self, authentic, and clear, then you've succeeded. The scenes/stories you've chosen throughout your story are meant to be there. At this point, everything you've chosen should connect and is there for a reason.

If you take the time to intertwine with your story and someone doesn't get it, then that's on them. Prince was so intertwined with his music and didn't worry about those who didn't or couldn't understand it. It rained the morning of the 2007 Halftime Show in Miami before Prince performed. After being alerted to storms, he responded to the production crew with "Can you make it rain harder?" Instead of being affected by what he couldn't change, he used the inclement weather to his advantage as a dramatic effect for his performance.

Reflection

Treat yourself with love and care as you hone in on where you want to go with your memoir. My advice: Put Prince on for inspiration

We're the experts of our own story, no matter how it was written, spoken, recorded, etc. Your dark night of the soul was NOT in vain. At this point, you've done everything you needed to do and its time to turn it over to publishing:

"The past has become your greatest asset."

—Big Book of Alcoholics Anonymous

Writing prompt

Reflect on what you've learned in the last 10 weeks of this journey. What are your major takeaways about how to craft your memoir? How comfortable are you with where you are in your writing journey?

_____

_____

_____

_____

_____

_____

_____

_____

_____

_____

_____

_____

_____

_____

"My passion is producing books true to the language of my heart. I created A-Team Press to connect other writers and dreamers with the resources I discovered to bring my books to life."

—Amy Liz Harrison
Author & CEO of A-Team Press